Journal of a Fossil Hunter

Chicago, Illinois

Raintree

Printed and bound in the United States by Lake Book
Manufacturing, Inc.

10 09 08 07 06
10 9 8 7 6 5 4 3 2 1

**Library of Congress Cataloging-in-
Publication Data**
Spilsbury, Louise.
  Journal of a fossil hunter : fossils / Louise and
Richard Spilsbury.
     p. cm.
  Includes bibliographical references.
  ISBN 1-4109-1923-4 (library binding) -- ISBN 1-
4109-1954-4 (pbk.)
  1. Fossils--Juvenile literature. 2. Paleontology--
Juvenile
literature. 3. Paleontologists--Juvenile literature. I.
Spilsbury, Richard.
II. Title.
  QE714.5.S645 2004
  560--dc22
                                                    2005009539

Acknowledgments
The author and publishers are grateful to the
following for permission to reproduce copyright
material: Comstock Images p. 5; Corbis pp. 5
(Royalty-Free), 14–15 (Royalty-Free), 22–23 (Royalty-
Free), 23 (Francis Latreille), 28 (Royalty-Free); EPSON
p. 5; Geoscience Features p. 7; Getty Images pp. 5
(PhotoDisc), 5 (PhotoDisc), 10–11 (PhotoDisc),
18–19 (PhotoDisc); Open University, Earth Science
Image Library p. 12–13; Oxford Scientific Films p. 4
(Co-Op/James Abke); Photri, INC pp. 15 , 29 TOP;
Robert Harding p. 19 (Rob Francis); Royal British
Columbia Museum p. 24–25; Science Photo Library
pp. 6–7 (Michael Marten), 8–9 (Christian Darkin),
10–11 (Sinclair Stammers), 16–17 (Christian Darkin),
20–21 (Christian Darkin), 26–27 (Emily Rayfield),
29 (Jim Amos).

Cover photograph of an ammonite in detail
reproduced with permission of Alamy (Brand
X Pictures).

The publishers would like to thank Nancy Harris
and Harold Pratt for their assistance in the
preparation of this book.

Every effort has been made to contact copyright
holders of any material reproduced in this book.
Any omissions will be rectified in subsequent
printings if notice is given to the publishers.

The paper used to print this book comes from
sustainable resources.

Disclaimer
All the Internet addresses (URLs) given in this book
were valid at the time of going to press. However,
due to the dynamic nature of the Internet, some
addresses may have changed, or sites may have
changed or ceased to exist since publication. While
the author and publishers regret any inconvenience
this may cause readers, no responsibility for any
such changes can be accepted by either the author
or the publishers.

Contents

Any words appearing in the text in bold, **like this**, are explained in the glossary. You can also look out for them in the word box at the bottom of each page.

Getting Started

I am going on a trip to look for **fossils**. I've been planning this trip for a long time. It took a while to get all my gear ready. Now, I'm on my way!

At last! I am▶
off on my trip.

fossils   record in rocks of animals and plants that lived in the past
prehistoric   the past, before written history

Some people think fossils are boring. But I'm on a real adventure. Fossils are a record of animals and plants that lived long ago. Fossils show us what life was like in **prehistoric** times. Prehistoric times were long before people could write and keep records.

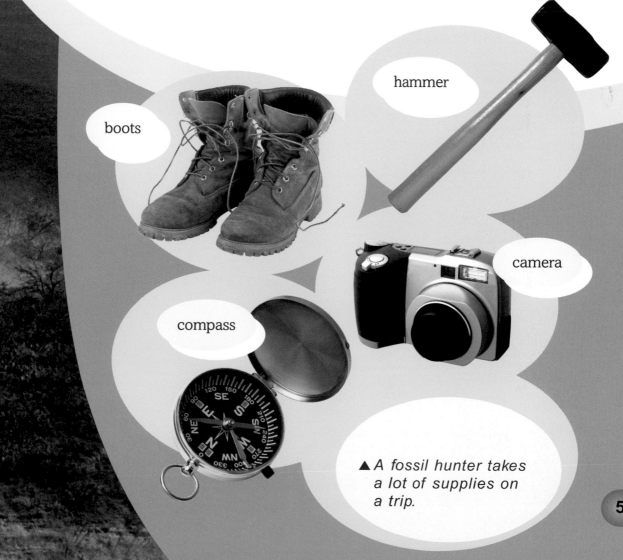

hammer

boots

camera

compass

▲ *A fossil hunter takes a lot of supplies on a trip.*

5

Blast from the Past

I found my first **fossil** today in a rock face. It's a fossil of an ammonite! Ammonites lived long ago in the sea.

When the ammonite died, its body sank to the seafloor. Slowly, the body was buried in **sediment**. Sediment is sand, mud, and broken shells. Slowly, the sediment pressed together and formed rock. This took millions of years.

The ammonite's soft body rotted away. Its hard shell became a fossil in the rock. The seawater is gone, but the fossil is still there.

Mold fossils and cast fossils

There are different types of fossil. A mold fossil is when there is an empty space in the shape of an animal or plant. A cast fossil is when stone fills the shape. The ammonite is a cast fossil.

6

sediment tiny pieces of rock or shell, such as sand or mud

◀ *A rock face like this one is a great place to find fossils.*

▼ *Fossils are usually the remains of hard parts of an animal, like this ammonite shell.*

This is what the seafloor ▼ may have looked like 400 million years ago.

When did ammonites die out?

Scientists can tell how old a type of rock is. Ammonite fossils are only found in rocks that are more than 65 million years old. This tells us that the ammonites died out 65 million years ago. They became **extinct**.

extinct   living thing that has completely died out

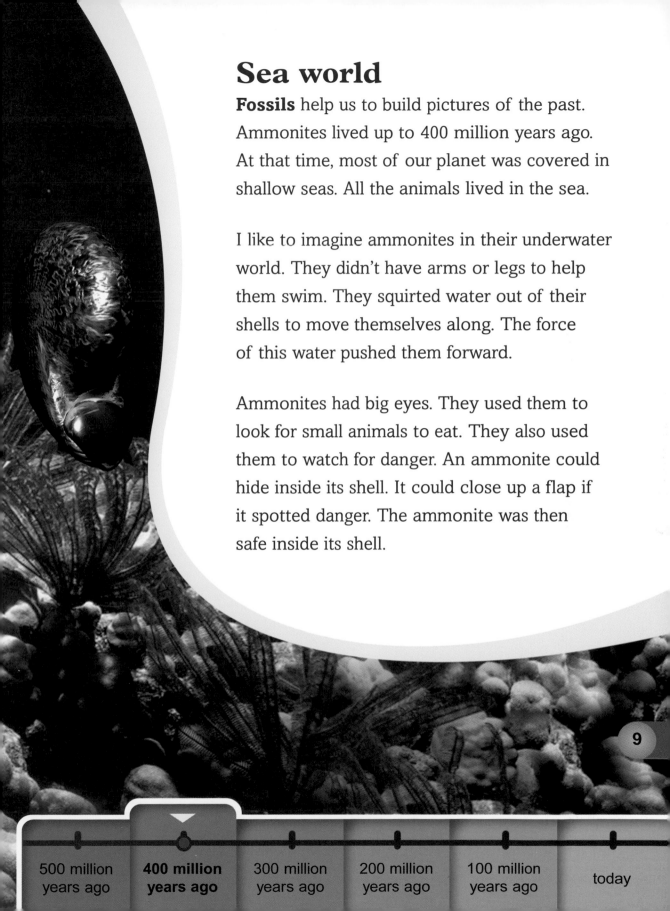

Sea world

Fossils help us to build pictures of the past. Ammonites lived up to 400 million years ago. At that time, most of our planet was covered in shallow seas. All the animals lived in the sea.

I like to imagine ammonites in their underwater world. They didn't have arms or legs to help them swim. They squirted water out of their shells to move themselves along. The force of this water pushed them forward.

Ammonites had big eyes. They used them to look for small animals to eat. They also used them to watch for danger. An ammonite could hide inside its shell. It could close up a flap if it spotted danger. The ammonite was then safe inside its shell.

500 million years ago | **400 million years ago** | 300 million years ago | 200 million years ago | 100 million years ago | today

Hunting in the Dark

I was hunting in a dark **coal** mine today. I tapped a rock and found **fossils** of fern leaves inside.

The fossils are the remains of fern plants that have now died out. They are **extinct**. The plants lived 300 million years ago. At this time, Earth was covered with forests of ferns. Some of the ferns were as tall as houses!

The fossils were formed after fern leaves fell to the ground. The leaves were trapped in mud, or **sediment**. Slowly, the sediment turned to rock. The leaves inside were pressed flat. They slowly turned into a thin layer of coal. That's why the fern fossil looks shiny and dark.

These fossils were▶ made by delicate fern leaves.

coal   soft, black rock that is burned to make heat or power

Coal forests

Most dead fern leaves rotted away.
They turned into a soft, black sludge.
Slowly, this sludge turned into coal.
This took millions of years.

This is how a prehistoric ▼ fern forest may have looked. It would have smelled like rotting leaves and buzzed with the sound of insects.

amphibian animal that spends part of its life in water and part on land

Weird forests

We know that giant ferns in the past probably grew in swampy areas. We know this because ferns today grow on damp land. The **fossils** found in **coal** help us to picture the past. Earth started to get warmer 300 million years ago. Things changed on Earth. Seas dried up and left swampy land behind. Plants grew quickly in these swampy areas. Animals began to live in the forests near the sea.

The **prehistoric** forest was steamy and dark. It was crowded with giant ferns and mosses. There were huge dragonflies. They were the length of a baseball bat. Huge fish swam in the dark pools among the plants. Frogs and other **amphibians** crawled across the land. Amphibians can live on land and in water. Some amphibians were the length of an alligator!

| 500 million years ago | 400 million years ago | **300 million years ago** | 200 million years ago | 100 million years ago | today |

Digging Dinosaurs

I am in the desert now. I found this **fossil** skull a few hours ago. It took me a long time to dig it from the rock.

It is the skull of a **dinosaur** called *Daspletosaurus*. ("dass-pleeto-sore-us"). Dinosaurs have all died out. They are **extinct**. Dinosaurs are the relatives of crocodiles and lizards. *Daspletosaurus* was a big **predator**. It hunted, killed, and ate other animals.

There were other bones nearby. They are from different dinosaurs that died around the same time.

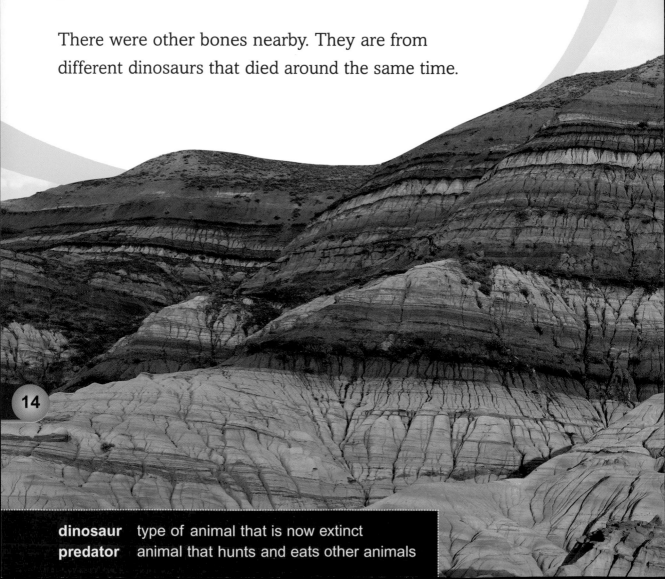

14

dinosaur type of animal that is now extinct
predator animal that hunts and eats other animals

▲*This dinosaur's teeth were almost 5 inches (12 centimeters) long!*

The Daspletosaurus ▼ *probably had no time to feed before the other dinosaurs took its meal.*

16

asteroid   rock that falls to Earth from space
prey   animal that is eaten by other animals

Dinosaur kill

I found other bones near the *Daspletosaurus* skull. Some of these bones were from a large, plant-eating **dinosaur**. The dinosaur was called *Triceratops* ("try-serra-tops"). Other bones were from smaller dinosaurs called *Troodons* ("troh-oh-dons").

What was the story behind all these bones? I can imagine the *Daspletosaurus* standing over its **prey**. It must have used its sharp teeth to kill the *Triceratops*. Maybe it was injured during the fight.

The fossils show that the *Troodons* died at the same time. Maybe the hungry *Troodons* heard the noisy fight. The *Troodons* could have worked together to attack the *Daspletosaurus*. This time, none of the dinosaurs survived.

Wipe out!

Dinosaurs died out, or became **extinct**, around 65 million years ago. This may have happened because a large **asteroid** hit Earth. Asteroids are large rocks that fall to Earth from space.

17

75 million years ago

| 500 million years ago | 400 million years ago | 300 million years ago | 200 million years ago | 100 million years ago | today |

On a Dig

I have found another **fossil**. This time I have uncovered a complete skeleton. It is from an animal that looked like a guinea pig. Yet it was the size of a buffalo! Its name is *Phoberomys* ("fobber-oh-miss"). Fossil hunters call it "Guinea-zilla."

The teeth in Guinea-zilla's skull show that it ate plants. It used its long front teeth for biting through leaves. It used its flat back teeth to chew the leaves.

Today, the place where I found Guinea-zilla is covered in sand. Yet eight million years ago, there was a shallow river here. Guinea-zilla ate the plants that grew along the riverbank.

Trace fossils

It's rare to find a complete fossil skeleton. Most fossils are of small seashells. Other fossils are single bones or teeth. Some fossils are of footprints, burrows, or droppings. These are called **trace fossils**.

trace fossils   fossil footprints, burrows, or droppings

▼ It is very rare to find a complete fossil skeleton. Most fossils are single bones such as this one.

Tale from the riverbank

Guinea-zilla was big, but it had many **predators**. Predators are animals that hunt and eat other animals. There are **fossils** of other animals that lived on the riverbank. There were huge crocodiles in the water. There were giant birds in the tall grasses.

This is how Guinea-zilla may ▶ have looked. It was up to 10 feet (3 meters) long.

Ancestors

*Guinea-zilla is an **ancestor** of guinea pigs. This means that the guinea-zilla is related to guinea-pigs, but it lived in the past. The shapes of its skeleton and teeth are like a guinea pig's skeleton and teeth.*

20

ancestor   living thing that is related to another living thing at a later point in time

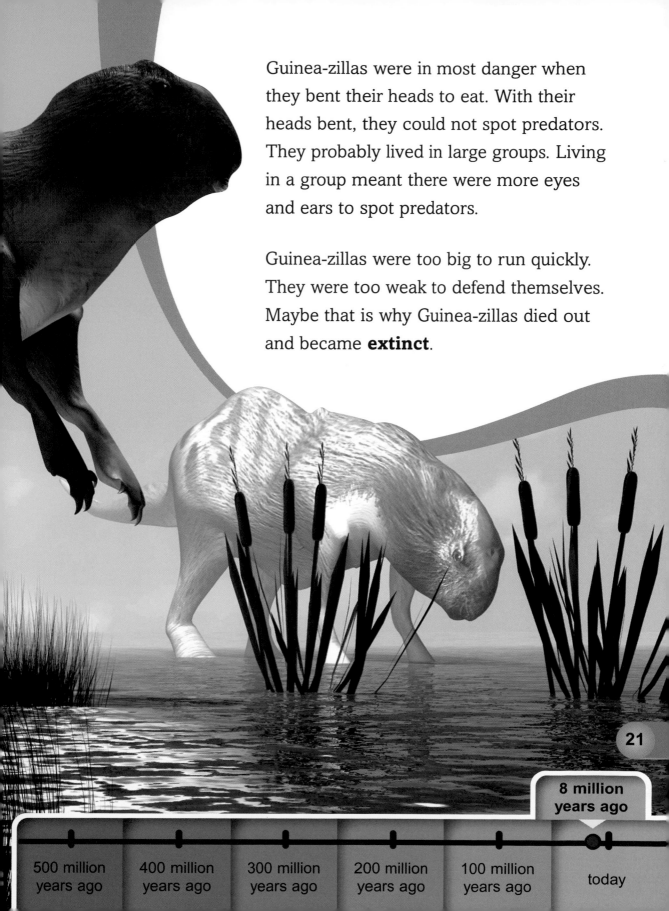

Guinea-zillas were in most danger when they bent their heads to eat. With their heads bent, they could not spot predators. They probably lived in large groups. Living in a group meant there were more eyes and ears to spot predators.

Guinea-zillas were too big to run quickly. They were too weak to defend themselves. Maybe that is why Guinea-zillas died out and became **extinct**.

21

8 million years ago

| 500 million years ago | 400 million years ago | 300 million years ago | 200 million years ago | 100 million years ago | today |

Frozen in Time

I can hardly feel my fingers as I write this diary. I have been chipping away at solid, frozen soil. I have found something different from a **fossil**. Forget about bones in rocks— I have found a whole, frozen animal!

Frozen remains

Some animal remains are found in ice. Some of these remains are in very good condition. They are in good condition because they stayed cold all the time. They would have begun to rot if they had warmed up.

◄This is the foot of the woolly mammoth. It has been buried in ice for 20,000 years. Yet it looks like it died only yesterday.

The animal is a woolly mammoth. Mammoths are **extinct**. They died out long ago. They looked like huge elephants with long, reddish hair. My frozen mammoth looks very much like it did when it was alive. You can even see the wrinkles on the skin of its feet!

What is an Ice Age?

Today, ice covers Earth near the North and South Poles. Ice covered more of Earth 20,000 years ago. The **climate** was so cold that many animals died out and became **extinct**. This part of Earth's history is called the Ice Age.

24

climate   usual pattern of weather over a long time

Ice-Age jumbo

Mammoths lived during the Ice Age. The world was covered in ice and snow during the Ice Age. The plants that mammoths ate were buried underneath the snow. Mammoths used their tusks to scrape away the snow.

Woolly mammoths are the **ancestors** of elephants. They are related to elephants but lived long ago. Both animals have a trunk, tusks, flapping ears, and thick legs. The mammoth's ears were smaller than an elephant's ears. The mammoth's tusks were curlier than an elephant's tusks, too.

I wonder how my mammoth died. Maybe it fell into a crack in the ice and couldn't get out?

◀ *A mammoth had a thick coat of hair to keep it warm.*

20,000 years ago

500 million years ago	400 million years ago	300 million years ago	200 million years ago	100 million years ago	today

Pictures of the Past

It's the end of the trip and the last page of my diary. Yet my work is not over. My **fossil** finds are like pieces of a jigsaw puzzle. I can use them to make a picture of the past.

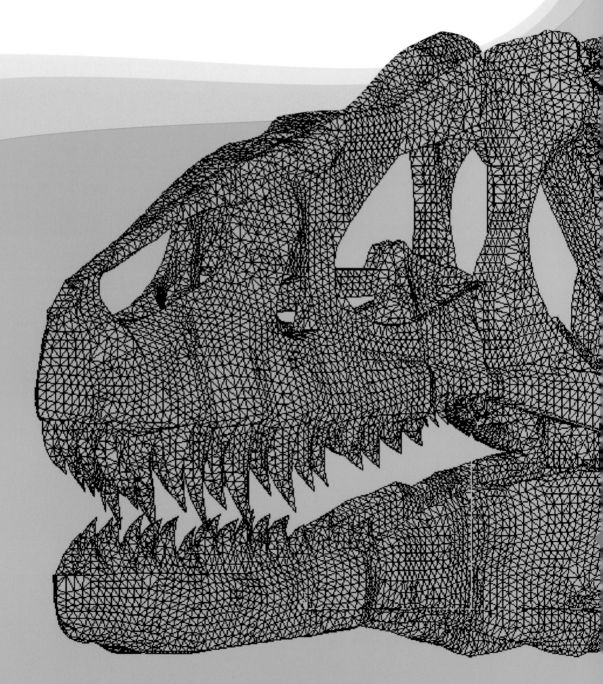

Fossils are clues about **prehistoric** times. They tell us about plants and animals from the past. Many of the plants and animals from the past are different from their modern relatives. Fossils can show us what the **ancestors** of today's plants and animals were like.

Fossils also show how Earth's surface has changed. For example, we know that some dry land today was once under the sea. We know this because we have found fossils of ammonites.

The fossils in my diary only tell part of the story of life on Earth. There are many more fossils to find. Why don't you try to find some fossils, too?

◄A computer can make a model of an **extinct** animal from a few fossil bones. This picture shows the head of a **dinosaur**.

Filling in the Gaps

This timeline shows some of the things that have lived on Earth between 500 million years ago and today. People use **fossils** to make timelines like this.

250 million years ago

Earliest **dinosaur** footprint.

500 million years ago

400 million years ago

300 million years ago

500 million years ago

Fossils of fish show that much of Earth was covered by seas.

400 million years ago

Fossils of ammonites tell us that these animals were living in the sea.

300 million years ago

Fern fossil shows that plants were growing in swamps.

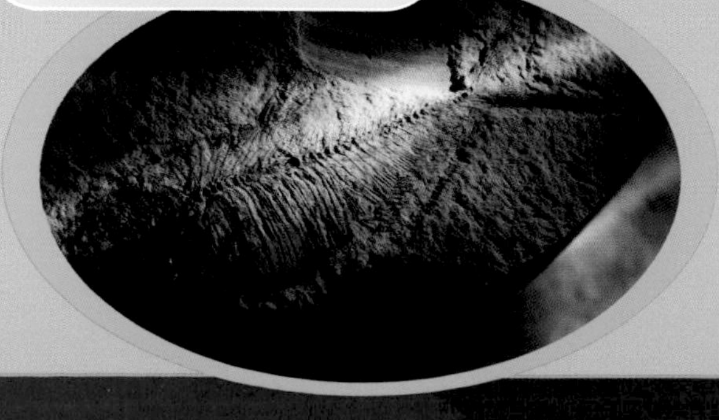

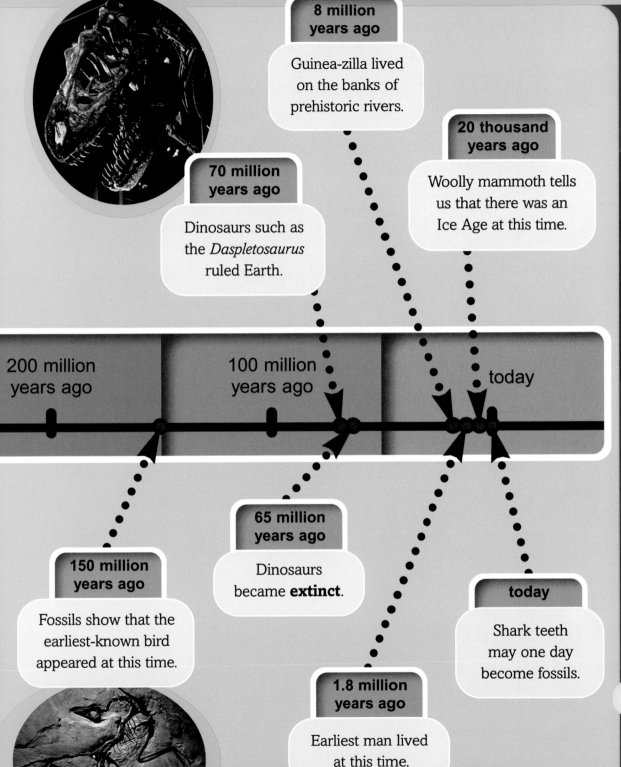

8 million years ago

Guinea-zilla lived on the banks of prehistoric rivers.

70 million years ago

Dinosaurs such as the *Daspletosaurus* ruled Earth.

20 thousand years ago

Woolly mammoth tells us that there was an Ice Age at this time.

200 million years ago

100 million years ago

today

150 million years ago

Fossils show that the earliest-known bird appeared at this time.

65 million years ago

Dinosaurs became **extinct**.

1.8 million years ago

Earliest man lived at this time.

today

Shark teeth may one day become fossils.

Glossary

amphibian animal that spends part of its life in water and part on land. Frogs, toads, and newts are modern amphibians.

ancestor living thing that is related to another living thing at a later point in time. The woolly mammoth was an ancestor of the modern elephant.

asteroid rock that falls to Earth from space. An asteroid may have wiped out the dinosaurs.

climate usual pattern of weather over a long time. The climate on Earth has changed through history.

coal soft, black rock that is burned to make heat or power

dinosaur type of animal that is now extinct. *Daspletosaurus*, *Triceratops*, and *Troodon* are types of dinosaur.

extinct living thing that has completely died out. Dinosaurs and ammonites are extinct animals.

fossil record in rocks of animals and plants that lived in the past

predator animal that hunts and eats other animals. *Daspletosaurus* was a predator.

prehistoric the past, before written history. Dinosaurs lived in prehistoric times.

prey animal that is eaten by other animals. *Phoberomys* was the prey of many animals.

sediment tiny pieces of rock or shells. Sand and mud are two types of sediment.

trace fossils fossil footprints, burrows, or droppings. Trace fossils show what an animal did when it was alive.

Fossil names

ammonite say "ammo-night"

Daspletosaurus say "dass-pleet-o-sore-us"

Phoberomys say "fobber-oh-miss"

Triceratops say "try-serra-tops"

Troodon say "troh-oh-don"

Want to Know More?

There's lots to know about fossil hunting! These are the best places to look:

Books

- Arnold, Caroline. *When Mammoths Walked the Earth*. Boston: Houghton Mifflin, 2002.
- Oxlade, Chris. *The Mystery of the Death of the Dinosaurs*. Chicago: Heinemann Library, 2002.
- Stewart, Melissa. *Fossils*. Chicago: Heinemann Library, 2002.

Websites

- http://www.fieldmuseum.org/sue/index.html
  Check out this exciting website to learn about Sue, the largest *Tyrannosaurus rex* fossil ever discovered. You can also make a cool dinosaur flip book! Sponsored by the Field Museum.
- http://www.sdnhm.org/kids/dinosaur/
  Do you want to learn more about dinosaurs and fossils? Visit this cool website to find out more information while playing games and solving puzzles! Sponsored by the San Diego Natural History Museum.

Ammonites weren't the only prehistoric sea animals to become fossils in rocks. Learn about the other sea animals in *Tales of a Prehistoric Sponge*.

The weather is one reason the surface of Earth has changed over time. Find out how in *The Disappearing Mountain and Other Earth Mysteries*.

31

Index